2ND EDITION

PIANO • VOCAL • GUITAR

ULTIMATE

COUNTRY

T0051138

ISBN 0-7935-4280-4

HAL•LEONARD®
CORPORATION

7777 W. BLUEMOUND RD. P.O.BOX 13819 MILWAUKEE, WI 53213

Visit Hal Leonard Online at
www.halleonard.com

CONTENTS

• 90 OF THE BEST •

ACHY BREAKY HEART
(Don't Tell My Heart)

Words and Music by
DON VON TRESS

Steady beat

mf

You can tell the world you
You can tell your ma I

nev - er was my girl. ___
moved to Ark - an - sas. ___

You can burn my clothes when I'm
You can tell your dog to bite my

gone.
leg.

Or you can tell your friends ___ just
Or tell your broth - er Cliff ___ whose

9

ACT NATURALLY

Words and Music by VONIE MORRISON
and JOHNNY RUSSELL

ev - er hit the big - time.

And all I got - ta do is

act nat - 'ral - ly.

We'll

ALL MY EX'S LIVE IN TEXAS

Words and Music by LYNDIA J. SHAFER
and SANGER D. SHAFER

16

ALL THE GOLD IN CALIFORNIA

Words and Music by
LARRY GATLIN

All The Gold In Cal-i-for-nia__ is in a__ bank in the mid-dle of Bev-er-ly Hills__ in some-bod-y el-se's__ name. So if you're__ dream-in'__ a-bout Cal-i-for-nia,__

MCA Music Publishing

ALWAYS ON MY MIND

Words and Music by WAYNE THOMPSON,
MARK JAMES and JOHNNY CHRISTOPHER

22

AMERICAN MADE

Words and Music by BOB DiPIERO
and PAT McMANUS

Seems ev'-ry-thing you buy these days_ has got a for-eign name;_
She looks good in her tight blue jeans_ she bought in Mex - i - co;_

From the kind of car_ I drive,_ to my vid-e-o_ game;_
And she loves wear-in' French per - fume,_ ev'-ry-where we_ go;_

I've got a Ni-kon cam - era, a Son-y col-or T. V.;_
But when it comes to the lov-in' part,_ one thing is true;_

ANGEL OF THE MORNING

Words and Music by
CHIP TAYLOR

There'll be no strings to bind your hands,___ not if my love can't bind your
May-be the sun's light will __ be dim,____ and it won't mat - ter an - y -

heart;
how;

and there's no need to take a
if morn-ing's ech - o says we've

stand __ for it was I who chose to start.
sinned, well, it was what I want-ed now.

ANY DAY NOW

Words and Music by BOB HILLIARD
and BURT BACHARACH

ANY TIME

Words and Music by
HERBERT HAPPY LAWSON

THE BATTLE HYMN OF LOVE

Words and Music by DON SCHLITZ
and PAUL OVERSTREET

MCA Music Publishing

40

THE BEACHES OF CHEYENNE

Words and Music by BRYAN KENNEDY,
GARTH BROOKS and DAN ROBERTS

wa - ter, you'll see her foot-prints in the sand. 'Cause ev - 'ry

night she walks the beach - es of Chey - enne.

Yes, ev - 'ry night she walks the beach - es of Chey -

enne.

rit.

BLUE BAYOU

Words and Music by ROY ORBISON
and JOE MELSON

BLUE EYES CRYING IN THE RAIN

Words and Music by
FRED ROSE

53

BRAND NEW MAN

Words and Music by DON COOK,
RONNIE DUNN and KIX BROOKS

BLUE MOON OF KENTUCKY

Words and Music by
BILL MONROE

62

63

BOOT SCOOTIN' BOOGIE

Words and Music by
RONNIE DUNN

night when the sun ___ goes down. ___ They got whis-
and let the hors - es run. ___ I go fly-
(Solo)
hot - ter than the Fourth of Ju - ly. ___ I see out -

- key, wom - en, ___ mu - sic and smoke. ___ It's
in' down that high - way to that hide - a - way ___
(Solo)
- laws, in - laws, ___ crooks ___ and straights ___

where all the cow - boy folk ___ go to boot scoot - in'
stuck out in the woods, to do the boot scoot - in'
(Solo)
all out ___ mak - in' it shake do - in' the boot scoot - in'

1, 3   **2, 4**

boo - gie. ___ I've
boo - gie. ___
(Solo)   *Solo ends* The
boo - gie. ___ Yeah, __

heel to toe, do - cie doe, come on ba - by, let's go

boot scoot-in'! Woh, __ Cad - il - lac, Black - jack,

ba - by meet me out back, we're gon - na boo - gie.

Oh, __ get down turn a - round, __ go to town, __ boot scoot-in'

BY THE TIME I GET TO PHOENIX

Words and Music by
JIMMY WEBB

CAN'T HELP FALLING IN LOVE

Words and Music by GEORGE DAVID WEISS,
HUGO PERETTI and LUIGI CREATORE

THE CHAIR

Words and Music by HANK COCHRAN
and DEAN DILLON

COLD, COLD HEART

Words and Music by
HANK WILLIAMS

81

CHARLOTTE'S WEB

Words and Music by JOHN DURRILL,
CLIFF CROFFORD and SNUFF GARRETT

CHATTAHOOCHEE

Words and Music by JIM McBRIDE
and ALAN JACKSON

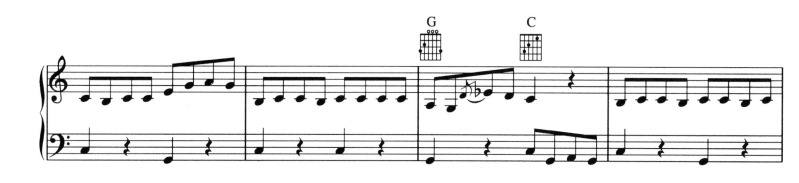

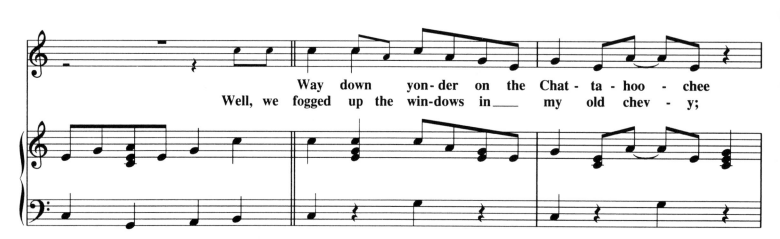

Way down yon-der on the Chat-ta-hoo - chee

Well, we fogged up the win-dows in____ my old chev-y;

lot a - bout liv - in' and a lit - tle 'bout ___ love.

COULD I HAVE THIS DANCE

Words and Music by WAYLAND HOLYFIELD
and BOB HOUSE

Moderately Slow

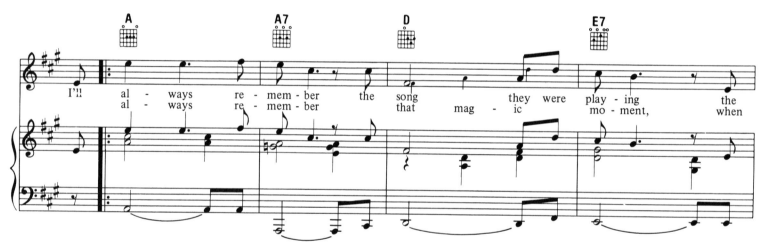

I'll al - ways re - mem - ber the song they were play - ing, the
al - ways re - mem - ber that mag - ic mo - ment, when

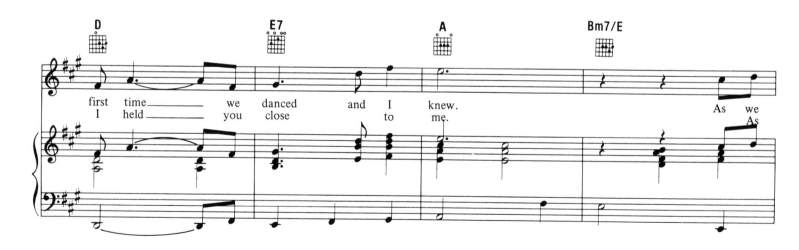

first time we danced and I knew.
I held you close to me.

As we
As

DISTANT DRUMS

Words and Music by
CINDY WALKER

CRAZY

Words and Music by
WILLIE NELSON

CRYIN' TIME

Words and Music by
BUCK OWENS

Now they say that ab-sence makes the heart grow fon-der,___ And that tears are on-ly rain to make love grow

Well, my love for you could nev-er grow no strong-er,___ If I lived to be a hund-red years

old. Oh, it's cry-in' time a-gain, you're gon-na leave me,___ I can see that far a-way look ___ in your

DOWN AT THE TWIST AND SHOUT

Words and Music by
MARY CHAPIN CARPENTER

Fast Country two-beat

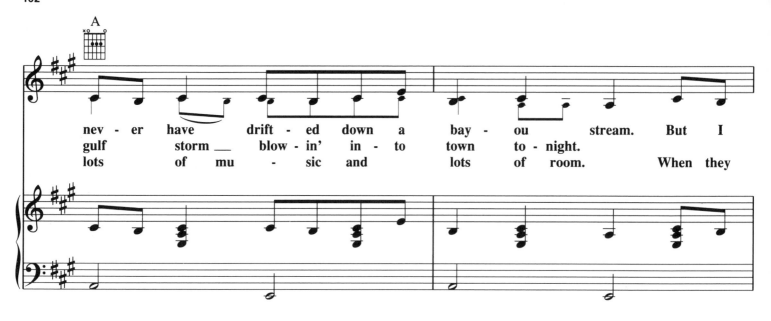

nev - er have drift - ed down a bay - ou stream. But I
gulf storm __ blow - in' in - to town to - night.
lots of mu - sic and lots of room. When they

heard that mu - sic on the ra - di - o, and I __
Liv - in' on the del - ta it's quite __ a show. __ They got hur -
play you a waltz from a nine - teen ten, you're

swore some - day I was gon - na go: __ down a - high - way 10, past a
- ri - cane par - ties ev - 'ry time it blows. __ But here up north __ it's a
gon - na feel a lit - tle bit young a - gain. __ Well you learn to dance __ with your

DREAM BABY
(How Long Must I Dream)

Words and Music by
CINDY WALKER

ELVIRA

Words and Music by
DALLAS FRAZIER

112

Verse 2. Tonight I'm gonna meet her
At the hungry house cafe
And I'm gonna give her all the love I can
She's gonna jump and holler
'Cause I saved up my last two dollar
And we're gonna search and find that preacher man
Chorus

FADED LOVE

Words and Music by BOB WILLS
and JOHNNY WILLS

Moderato

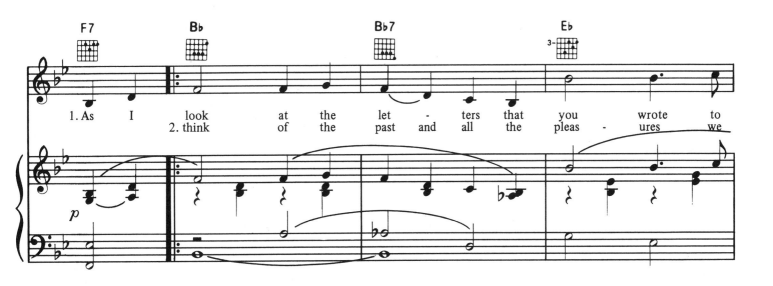

1. As I look at the let - ters that you wrote to me
2. think of the past and all the pleas - ures we

me It's you that I'm think - ing of,
had As I watch the mat - ing of the dove,

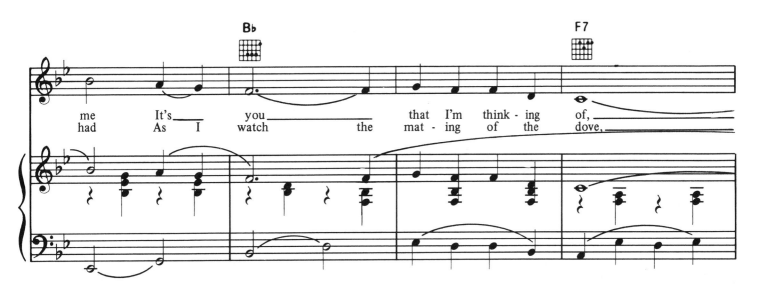

FLOWERS ON THE WALL

Words and Music by
LEWIS DeWITT

Moderato

1. I've been hear-in' you're con-cerned_ a - bout my hap-pi-ness;_
night I dressed_ in tails, pre-tend-ed I was on the town;_
good to see_ you, I must go,_ I know I look a fright;_

But all that thought_ you're giv-in' me_ is
As long as I _ can dream it's hard_ to
An - y way_ my eyes are not_ ac -

118

FOR THE GOOD TIMES

Words and Music by
KRIS KRISTOFFERSON

Don't look so sad; _____ I know it's o-ver; _____
long; _____ you'll find an-oth-er; _____

But life goes on _____ and this old world _____ will keep on
And I'll be here _____ if you should find _____ you ev-er

turn-ing. _____ Let's just be glad _____ we had some
need me. _____ Don't say a word _____ a-bout to-

FOLSOM PRISON BLUES

Words and Music by
JOHN R. CASH

Moderately (not too slow)

Chorus

1. I

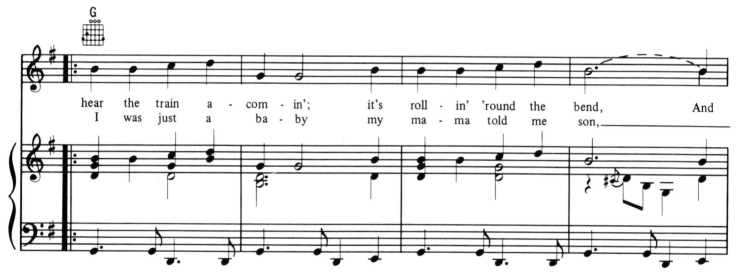

hear the train a - com - in'; it's roll - in' 'round the bend, And
I was just a ba - by my ma - ma told me son,_____

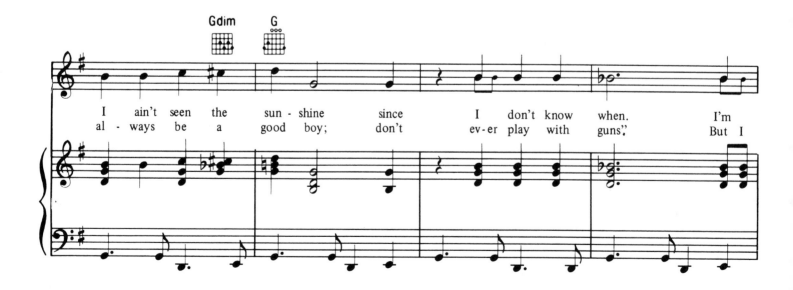

I ain't seen the sun - shine since I don't know when. I'm
al - ways be a good boy; don't ev - er play with guns", But I

123

3. I bet there's rich folks eatin' in a fancy dining car.
They're prob'ly drinkin' coffee and smokin' big cigars,
But I know I had it comin', I know I can't be free,
But those people keep a-movin', and that's what tortures me.

4. Well, if they freed me from this prison, if that railroad train was mine,
I bet I'd move on over a little farther down the line,
Far from Folsom Prison, that's where I want to stay,
And I'd let that lonesome whistle blow my blues away.

FRIENDS IN LOW PLACES

Words and Music by DEWAYNE BLACKWELL
and EARL BUD LEE

FROM GRACELAND TO THE PROMISED LAND

Words and Music by
MERLE HAGGARD

THE GAMBLER

Words and Music by
DON SCHLITZ

136

GENTLE ON MY MIND

Words and Music by
JOHN HARTFORD

2. It's not clinging to the rocks and ivy planted on their columns now that binds me
Or something that somebody said because they thought we fit together walkin'.
It's just knowing that the world will not be cursing or forgiving when I walk along
Some railroad track and find
That you're moving on the backroads by the rivers of my memory and for hours
You're just gentle on my mind.

3. Though the wheat fields and the clothes lines and junkyards and the highways
Come between us
And some other woman crying to her mother 'cause she turned and I was gone.
I still run in silence, tears of joy might stain my face and summer sun might
Burn me 'til I'm blind
But not to where I cannot see you walkin' on the backroads by the rivers flowing
Gentle on my mind.

4. I dip my cup of soup back from the gurglin' cracklin' caldron in some train yard
My beard a roughning coal pile and a dirty hat pulled low across my face.
Through cupped hands 'round a tin can I pretend I hold you to my breast and find
That you're waving from the backroads by the rivers of my memory ever smilin'
Ever gentle on my mind.

GREEN GREEN GRASS OF HOME

Words and Music by
CURLY PUTMAN

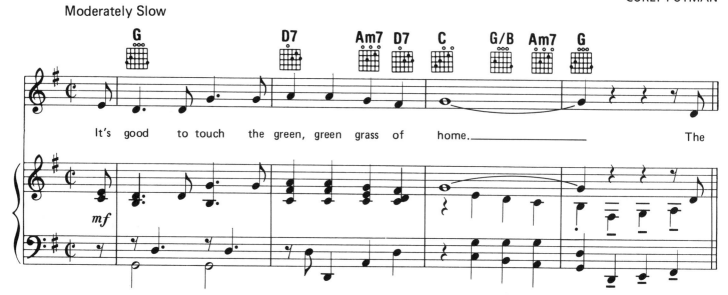

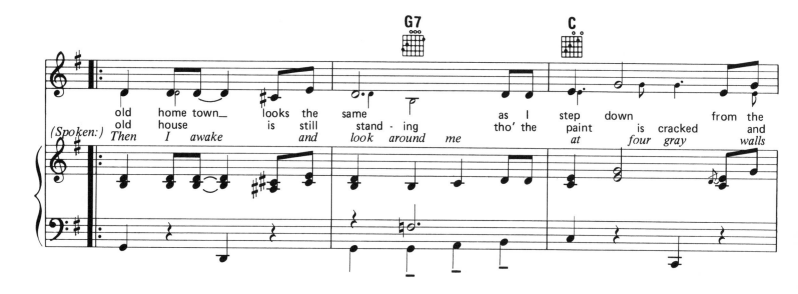

GUITAR MAN

By JERRY REED

Well, I quit my job down at the car wash, I left my
starved to death down in Mem - phis ___ I
trip down to the o - cean find your -

ma - ma a good - bye note. By sun - down I'd left
run out of mon - ey and luck. So, I bummed me a ride down to
self down a - round Mo - bile, well, make it on out to the

King - ston with ___ my gui - tar un - der my
Ma - con, Geor - gia on a o - ver - load - ed poul - try
club called Jack's ___ if you got a lit - tle time ___ to

146

THE HAPPIEST GIRL
IN THE WHOLE U.S.A.

Words and Music by
DONNA FARGO

HARD ROCK BOTTOM
OF YOUR HEART

Words and Music by
HUGH PRESTWOOD

HEY, GOOD LOOKIN'

Words and Music by
HANK WILLIAMS

162

HE'LL HAVE TO GO

Words and Music by JOE ALLISON
and AUDREY ALLISON

HERE YOU COME AGAIN

Words by CYNTHIA WEIL
Music by BARRY MANN

Here you come a-gain, ____ just when I've ____ be-gun to get my-
Here you come a-gain, ____ just when I'm ____ a-bout to make it

self to-geth-er, you waltz right in the door, ____ just like you've done be-fore ____ and
work with-out you, you look in-to my eyes ____ and lie those pret-ty lies ____ and

wrap ____ my heart 'round your lit-tle fin-ger. pret-ty soon ____ I'm wond-'rin ____ how I

171

I BELIEVE IN YOU

Words and Music by ROGER COOK
and SAM HOGIN

I CAN'T STOP LOVING YOU

Words and Music by
DON GIBSON

I FALL TO PIECES

Words and Music by HANK COCHRAN
and HARLAN HOWARD

I FEEL LUCKY

Words and Music by MARY CHAPIN CARPENTER
and DON SCHLITZ

woke up this morn - ing, stum - bled out of my rack. ___ I o -
strolled down to the cor - ner, gave my num - bers to the clerk. The pot's __
lev - en mil - lion lat - er, I was sit - tin' at the bar. I bought __

186

I JUST FALL IN LOVE AGAIN

Words and Music by LARRY HERBSTRITT, STEPHEN H. DORFF,
GLORIA SKLEROV and HARRY LLOYD

I WALK THE LINE

Words and Music by
JOHN R. CASH

3. As sure as night is dark and day is light,
I keep you on my mind both day and night.
And happiness I've known proves that it's right.
Because you're mine I Walk The Line.

4. You've got a way to keep me on your side.
You give me cause for love that I can't hide.
For you I know I'd even try to turn the tide.
Because you're mine I Walk The Line.

5. I keep a close watch on this heart of mine.
I keep my eyes wide open all the time.
I keep the ends out for the tie that binds.
Because you're mine I Walk The Line.

I'LL STILL BE LOVING YOU

Words and Music by TODD CERNEY, PAM ROSE,
MARYANN KENNEDY and PAT BUNCH

MCA Music Publishing

I'll still be lov - in'___ you.

I'll still be lov - in', I'll still be lov - in' you.___

I'll still be lov - in' you._____

IT WAS ALMOST LIKE A SONG

Lyric by HAL DAVID
Music by ARCHIE JORDAN

Once in ev - 'ry life, some - one comes a -
You were in my arms, just where you be -

long, and you came to me.
long, we were so in love.

I'M SO LONESOME I COULD CRY

Words and Music by
HANK WILLIAMS

IT'S A HEARTACHE

Words and Music by RONNIE SCOTT
and STEVE WOLFE

204

THE KEEPER OF THE STARS

Words and Music by KAREN STALEY,
DANNY MAYO and DICKEY LEE

IT'S NOW OR NEVER

Words and Music by AARON SCHROEDER
and WALLY GOLD

KENTUCKY RAIN

Words and Music by EDDIE RABBITT
and DICK HEARD

213

LAST DATE

By FLOYD CRAMER

Slowly

216

KISS YOU ALL OVER

Words and Music by NICKY CHINN
and MIKE CHAPMAN

LAY DOWN SALLY

Words and Music by ERIC CLAPTON,
MARCY LEVY and GEORGE TERRY

Bright beat

There is noth-ing that ___ is wrong ___ in want-ing you ___ to stay ___
sun ain't near-ly on ___ the rise, ___ and we still got ___ the moon
long to see ___ the morn-ing light ___ col-or-ing ___ your face ___

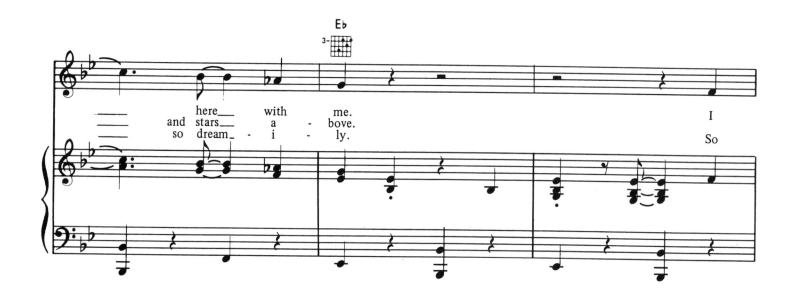

___ here ___ with me.
and stars ___ a-bove.
___ so dream-i-ly.

I
So

224

LONGNECK BOTTLE

Words and Music by RICK CARNES
and STEVE WARINER

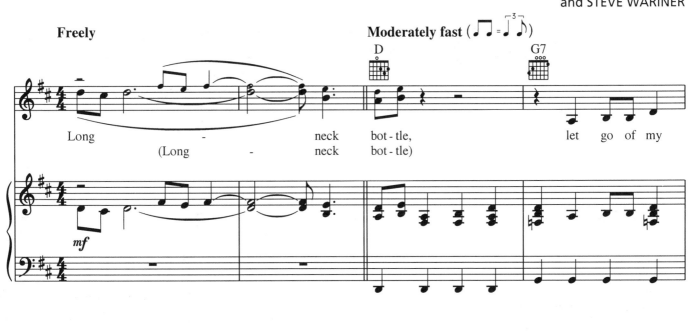

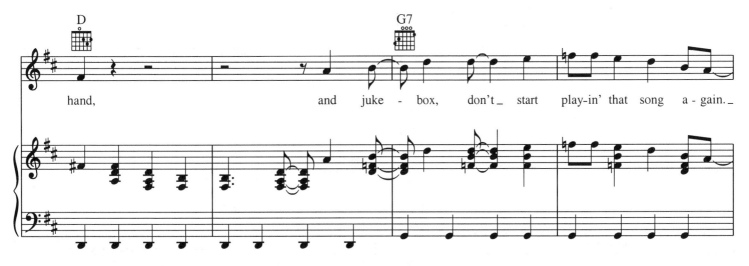

228

LOOKIN' FOR LOVE

Words and Music by WANDA MALLETTE,
PATTI RYAN and BOB MORRISON

232

NEON MOON

Words and Music by
RONNIE DUNN

238

LUCILLE

Words and Music by ROGER BOWLING
and HAL BYNUM

OH, LONESOME ME

Words and Music by
DON GIBSON

248

OKIE FROM MUSKOGEE

Words and Music by MERLE HAGGARD
and ROY EDWARD BURRIS

Moderately fast

Eb

1. We don't smoke mar-i-jua-na in Mus-ko-gee,
2. We don't make a par-ty out of lov-ing,
boots are still in style if a man needs foot-wear,

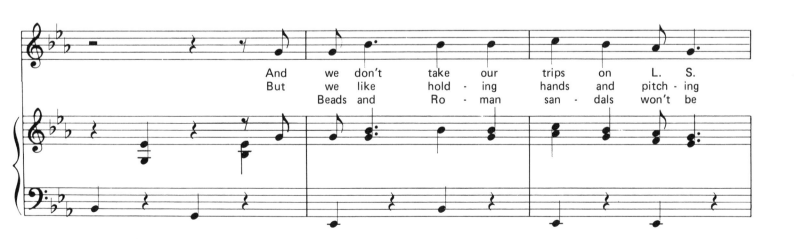

And we don't take our trips on L. S.
But we like hold-ing hands and pitch-ing
Beads and Ro-man san-dals won't be

250

place where e - ven squares can have a ball.____

We still wave Ol' Glo - ry down at the

Court House, White light - ning's still the

big - gest thrill of all.____ 3. Leath - er ____

A RAINY NIGHT IN GEORGIA

Words and Music by
TONY JOE WHITE

Additional Lyrics

3. I find me a place in a box car,
   So I take out my guitar to pass some time;
   Late at night when it's hard to rest,
   I hold your picture to my chest, and I'm all right;
   (To Chorus)

RING OF FIRE

Words and Music by MERLE KILGORE
and JUNE CARTER

Moderately Bright

Love _____ is a burn-ing thing _____

taste _____ of _ love is sweet _____

And it makes _____ a fi-ry

When_ hearts _____ like ours _

RELEASE ME

Words and Music by ROBERT YOUNT,
EDDIE MILLER and DUB WILLIAMS

SHAMELESS

Words and Music by
BILLY JOEL

Well, I'm shame-less when it comes to
shame-less Ba-by I don't

lov-ing you.___ I'd do an-y-thing you want me to. I'd do an-y-thing at
have a prayer. __ An-y-time I see you stand-ing there I go down up-on my

SHE IS HIS ONLY NEED

Words and Music by
DAVE LOGGINS

MCA Music Publishing

SHUT UP AND KISS ME

Words and Music by
MARY CHAPIN CARPENTER

Don't mean to get a lit- tle for- ward___ with you.
Did- n't ex- pect to be in this po- si- tion.
Come___ clos- er, ba- by, I can't___ hear you.

Don't mean to get a- head of
Did- n't ex- pect to have to
Just an- oth- er whis- per,

Talk is cheap and ba-by, time's ex-pen-sive. So why___ waste an-oth-er

SIXTEEN TONS

Words and Music by
MERLE TRAVIS

SNOWBIRD

Words and Music by
GENE MacLELLAN

284

TENNESSEE WALTZ

Words and Music by REDD STEWART
and PEE WEE KING

287

SOMEWHERE IN MY BROKEN HEART

Words and Music by BILLY DEAN
and RICHARD LEIGH

SOUTHERN NIGHTS

Words and Music by
ALLEN TOUSSAINT

Moderately with a beat

South - ern ___ nights, ___ have you ev - er felt a
South - ern ___ skies, ___ have you ev - er no - ticed

south - ern ___ night? ___ Free as a breeze, ___ not to
south - ern ___ skies? ___ Its pre - cious beau - ty lies

SUSPICIOUS MINDS

Words and Music by
MARK JAMES

SWEET DREAMS

Words and Music by
DON GIBSON

299

TAKE ME HOME, COUNTRY ROADS

Words and Music by JOHN DENVER,
BILL DANOFF and TAFFY NIVERT

THANK GOD I'M A COUNTRY BOY

Words and Music by
JOHN MARTIN SOMMERS

Moderately

Well, life on a farm is kind-a laid back, ain't
work's all ___ done and the sun's ___ settin' low I
wouldn't trade my life for dia-monds or jewels, I
fid-dle was my daddy's till the day he died, and he

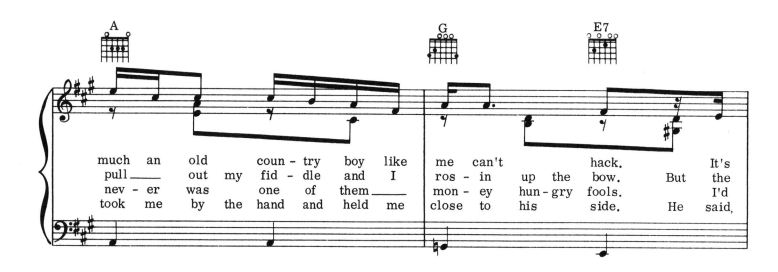

much an old coun-try boy like me can't hack. It's the
pull ___ out my fid-dle and I ros-in up the bow. But the
nev-er was one of them ___ mon-ey hun-gry fools. I'd
took me by the hand and held me close to his side. He said,

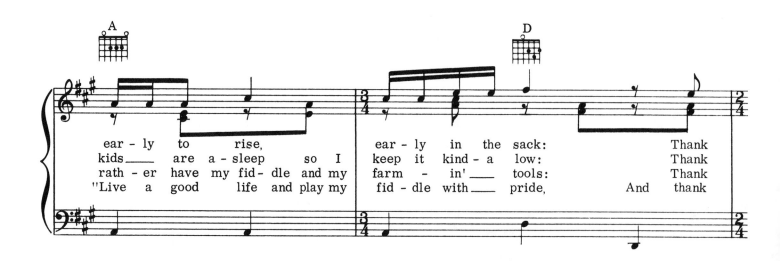

ear-ly to rise, ear-ly in the sack: Thank
kids ___ are a-sleep so I keep it kind-a low: Thank
rath-er have my fid-dle and my farm-in' ___ tools: Thank
"Live a good life and play my fid-dle with ___ pride, And thank

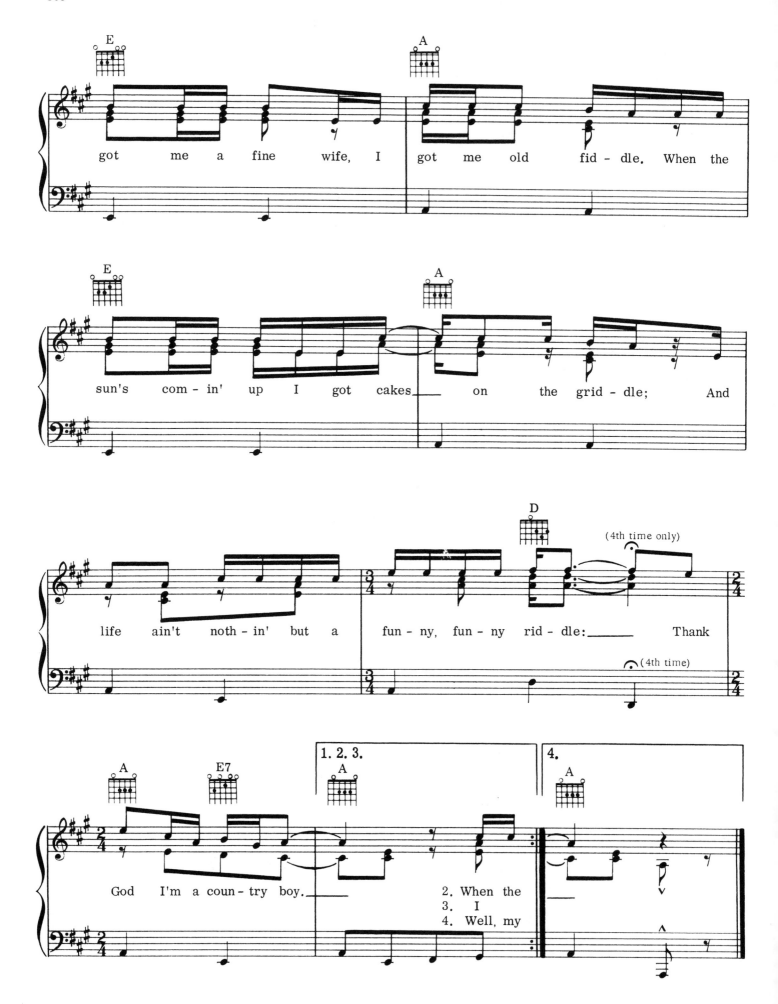

WHEN THE TINGLE BECOMES A CHILL

Words and Music by
LOLA JEAN DILLON

THERE'S A TEAR IN MY BEER

Words and Music by
HANK WILLIAMS

WALKIN' AFTER MIDNIGHT

Lyrics by DON HECHT
Music by ALAN W. BLOCK

WHEN SHE CRIES

Words and Music by MARC BEESON
and SONNY LeMAIRE

WHEN YOU SAY NOTHING AT ALL

Words and Music by DON SCHLITZ
and PAUL OVERSTREET

WHY NOT ME

Words and Music by HARLAN HOWARD,
SONNY THROCKMORTON and BRENT MAHER

326

WHY ME?
(Why Me, Lord?)

Words and Music by
KRIS KRISTOFFERSON

YOU DECORATED MY LIFE

Words and Music by DEBBIE HUPP
and BOB MORRISON

YOUR CHEATIN' HEART

Words and Music by
HANK WILLIAMS

THE ULTIMATE SERIES

This comprehensive series features jumbo collections of piano/vocal arrangements with guitar chords. Each volume features an outstanding selection of your favorite songs. Collect them all for the ultimate music library!

Blues

90 blues classics, including: Boom Boom • Born Under a Bad Sign • Gee Baby, Ain't I Good to You • I Can't Quit You Baby • Pride and Joy • (They Call It) Stormy Monday • Sweet Home Chicago • Why I Sing the Blues • You Shook Me • and more.
00310723 . . . .$19.95

Broadway Gold

100 show tunes: Beauty and the Beast • Do-Re-Mi • I Whistle a Happy Tune • The Lady Is a Tramp • Memory • My Funny Valentine • Oklahoma • Some Enchanted Evening • Summer Nights • Tomorrow • many more.
00361396 . . . .$21.95

Broadway Platinum

100 popular Broadway show tunes, featuring: Consider Yourself • Getting to Know You • Gigi • Do You Hear the People Sing • I'll Be Seeing You • My Favorite Things • People • She Loves Me • Try to Remember • Younger Than Springtime • many more.
00311496 . . . .$19.95

Children's Songbook

66 fun songs for kids: Alphabet Song • Be Our Guest • Bingo • The Brady Bunch • Do-Re-Mi • Hakuna Matata • It's a Small World • Kum Ba Yah • Sesame Street Theme • Tomorrow • Won't You Be My Neighbor? • and more.
00310690 . . . .$18.95

Christmas – Third Edition

Includes: Carol of the Bells • Deck the Hall • Frosty the Snow Man • Gesu Bambino • Good King Wenceslas • Jingle-Bell Rock • Joy to the World • Nuttin' for Christmas • O Holy Night • Rudolph the Red-Nosed Reindeer • Silent Night • What Child Is This? • and more.
00361399 . . . .$19.95

Classic Rock

70 rock classics in one great collection! Includes: Angie • Best of My Love • California Girls • Crazy Little Thing Called Love • I Love Rock'N'Roll • Joy to the World • Landslide • Light My Fire • Livin' on a Prayer • Mony, Mony • (She's) Some Kind of Wonderful • Sultans of Swing • Sweet Emotion • Werewolves of London • Wonderful Tonight • Ziggy Stardust • and more.
00310962 . . . .$22.95

Country – Second Edition

90 of your favorite country hits: Boot Scootin' Boogie • Chattahoochie • Could I Have This Dance • Crazy • Down at the Twist And Shout • Hey, Good Lookin' • Lucille • When She Cries • and more.
00310036 . . . .$19.95

Early Rock 'N' Roll

100 classics, including: All Shook Up • Bye Bye Love • Duke of Earl • Gloria • Hello Mary Lou • It's My Party • Johnny B. Goode • The Loco-Motion • Lollipop • Surfin' U.S.A. • The Twist • Wooly Bully • Yakety Yak • and more.
00361411 . . . .$21.95

Gospel

Includes: El Shaddai • His Eye Is on the Sparrow • How Great Thou Art • Just a Closer Walk With Thee • Lead Me, Guide Me • (There'll Be) Peace in the Valley (For Me) • Precious Lord, Take My Hand • Wings of a Dove • more.
00241009 . . . .$19.95

Jazz Standards

Over 100 great jazz favorites: Ain't Misbehavin' • All of Me • Come Rain or Come Shine • Here's That Rainy Day • I'll Take Romance • Imagination • Li'l Darlin' • Manhattan • Moonglow • Moonlight in Vermont • A Night in Tunisia • The Party's Over • Solitude • Star Dust • and more.
00361407 . . . .$19.95

Latin Songs

80 hot Latin favorites, including: Amapola (Pretty Little Poppy) • Amor • Bésame Mucho (Kiss Me Much) • Blame It on the Bossa Nova • Feelings (¿Dime?) • Malagueña • Mambo No. 5 • Perfidia • Slightly out of Tune (Desafinado) • What a Diff'rence a Day Made • more.
00310689 . . . .$19.95

Love and Wedding Songbook

90 songs of devotion including: The Anniversary Waltz • Canon in D • Endless Love • Forever and Ever, Amen • Just the Way You Are • Love Me Tender • Sunrise, Sunset • Through the Years • Trumpet Voluntary • and more!
00361445 . . . .$19.95

Movie Music

73 favorites from the big screen, including: Can You Feel the Love Tonight • Chariots of Fire • Cruella De Vil • Driving Miss Daisy • Easter Parade • Forrest Gump • Moon River • That Thing You Do! • Viva Las Vegas • The Way We Were • When I Fall in Love • and more.
00310240 . . . .$18.95

FOR MORE INFORMATION, SEE YOUR LOCAL MUSIC DEALER, OR WRITE TO:

HAL•LEONARD®
CORPORATION

7777 W. BLUEMOUND RD. P.O. BOX 13819 MILWAUKEE, WI 53213

http://www.halleonard.com

Prices, contents, and availability subject to change without notice.
Availability and pricing may vary outside the U.S.A.

Nostalgia Songs

100 great favorites from yesteryear, such as: Ain't We Got Fun? • Alexander's Ragtime Band • Casey Jones • Chicago • Danny Boy • Second Hand Rose • Swanee • Toot, Toot, Tootsie! • 'Way Down Yonder in New Orleans • The Yellow Rose of Texas • You Made Me Love You • and more!
00310730 . . . .$17.95

Pop/Rock

70 of the most popular pop/rock hits of our time, including: Bad, Bad Leroy Brown • Bohemian Rhapsody • Complicated • Drops of Jupiter (Tell Me) • Dust in the Wind • Every Little Thing She Does Is Magic • (Everything I Do) I Do It for You • From a Distance • I Don't Want to Wait • I Will Remember You • Imagine • Invisible Touch • More Than Words • Smooth • Tears in Heaven • Thriller • Walking in Memphis • You Are So Beautiful • and more.
00310963 . . . .$22.95

Singalong!

100 of the best-loved popular songs ever: Beer Barrel Polka • Crying in the Chapel • Edelweiss • Feelings • Five Foot Two, Eyes of Blue • For Me and My Gal • Indiana • It's a Small World • Que Sera, Sera • This Land Is Your Land • When Irish Eyes Are Smiling • and more.
00361418 . . . .$18.95

Standard Ballads

91 mellow masterpieces, including: Angel Eyes • Body and Soul • Darn That Dream • Day By Day • Easy to Love • Isn't It Romantic? • Misty • Mona Lisa • Moon River • My Funny Valentine • Smoke Gets in Your Eyes • When I Fall in Love • and more.
00310246 . . . .$19.95

Swing Standards

93 songs to get you swinging, including: Bandstand Boogie • Boogie Woogie Bugle Boy • Heart and Soul • How High the Moon • In the Mood • Moonglow • Satin Doll • Sentimental Journey • Witchcraft • and more.
00310245 . . . .$19.95

TV Themes

More than 90 themes from your favorite TV shows, including: The Addams Family Theme • Cleveland Rocks • Theme from Frasier • Happy Days • Love Boat Theme • Hey, Hey We're the Monkees • Nadia's Theme • Sesame Street Theme • Theme from Star Trek® • and more.
00310841 . . . .$19.95